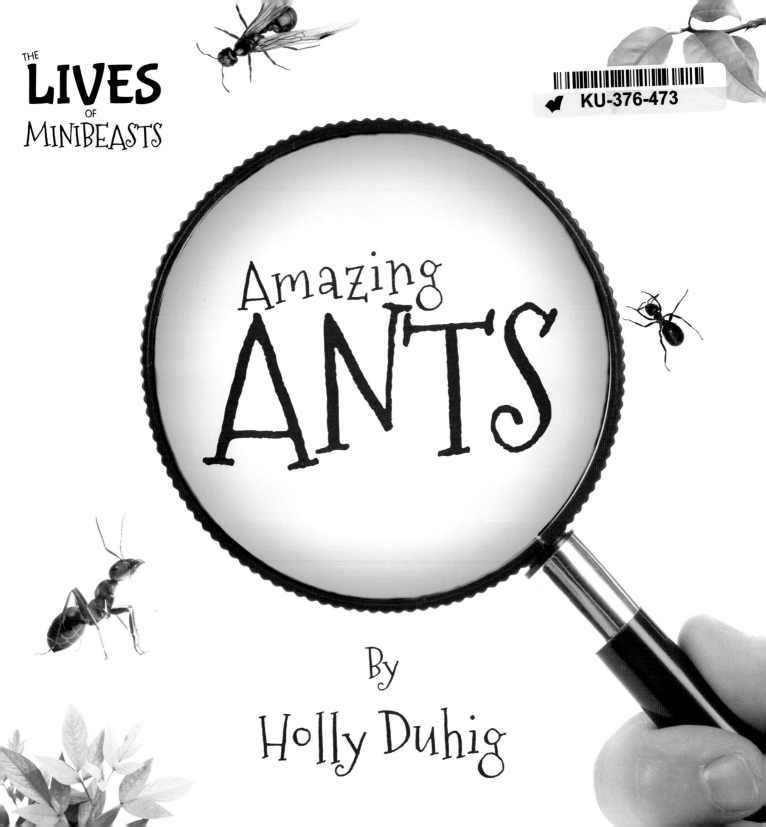

THE LIVES OF MINIBEASTS

Amazing ANTS

By Holly Duhig

©2017
Book Life
King's Lynn
Norfolk PE30 4LS

ISBN: 978-1-78637-187-4

All rights reserved
Printed in Malaysia

Written by:
Holly Duhig

Edited by:
Charlie Ogden

Designed by:
Danielle Jones

A catalogue record for this book
is available from the British Library

Photo Credits

CONTENTS

Words that look like **this** can be found in the glossary on page 24.

WHAT IS AN ANT?

Antennae

Ant Nest

An ant is an insect with six legs and two antennae. Ants live together in large groups called colonies. Ant colonies usually live in tunnels called nests.

All ant colonies have a queen ant. The queen is bigger than the other ants and her job is to lay eggs.

Queen Ant

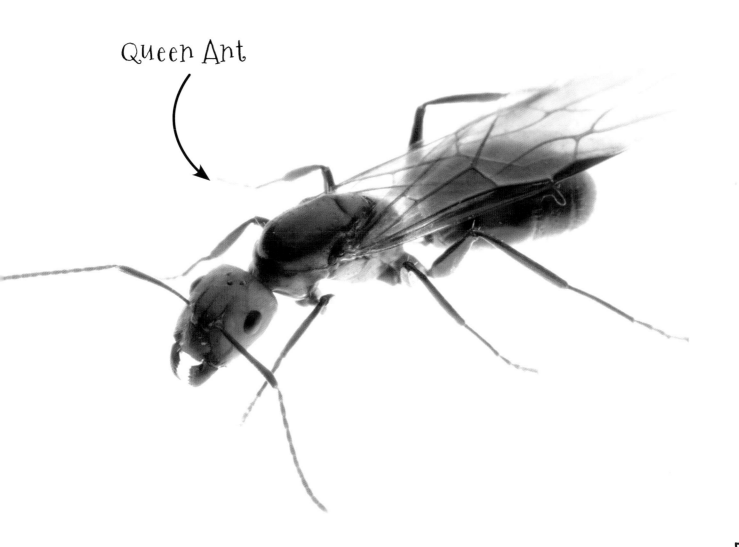

Mandibles

Fire ants are red in colour.

Ants are usually black or red. They have mandibles near their mouths that help them hold and cut up food.

Most ants are very small. Black garden ants are only three to five millimetres long, but their queens can grow up to nine millimetres long.

Queen Ant

Black
Garden Ant

HOW DO ANTS LAY EGGS?

A queen ant is born with wings. She uses these to fly around and find a **mate**. After she has found a mate, she can start laying eggs.

The queen ant digs deep into the ground to find a good place to lay her eggs and start a new colony. After this, she loses her wings.

Some queen ants can lay thousands of eggs in a single day.

ANT LARVAE

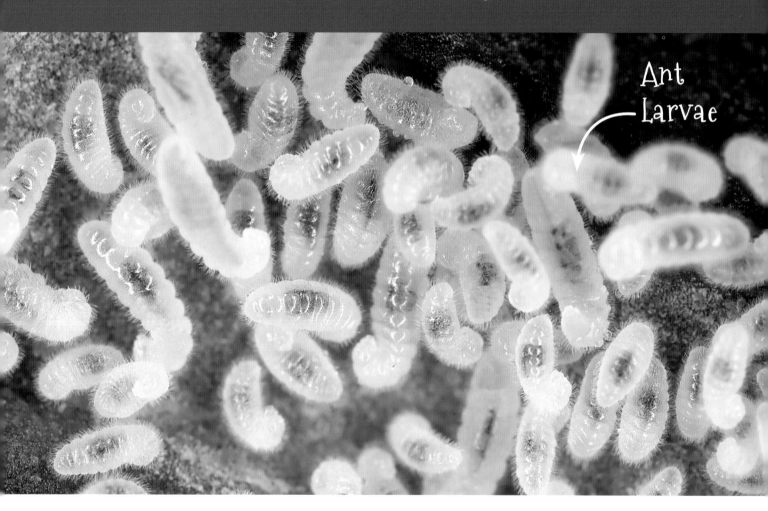

Ant Larvae

The queen's eggs hatch into **larvae**. Larvae look like small, white worms. The larvae will either become female ants, called workers, or male ants, called drones.

When a larva is old enough, it starts to make a **cocoon**. The cocoon helps to keep the larva safe while it turns into an adult ant.

WHERE DO ANTS LIVE?

Some ant nests go many metres under the ground.

Ants live in nests. Ant nests are usually made underground. They contain many **chambers** and tunnels.

Ants make their nests by carrying soil to the surface. This is why there are little mounds of soil at the top of ant's nests.

WHAT DO ANTS EAT?

Leafcutter ants can carry over 5,000 times their own body weight!

Different **species** of ant eat different things. Leafcutter ants bury chewed-up leaves in their nests. The ants then feed on the **fungus** that grows on the dead leaves.

Army ants hunt in big groups. They eat everything from small insects to snakes and lizards!

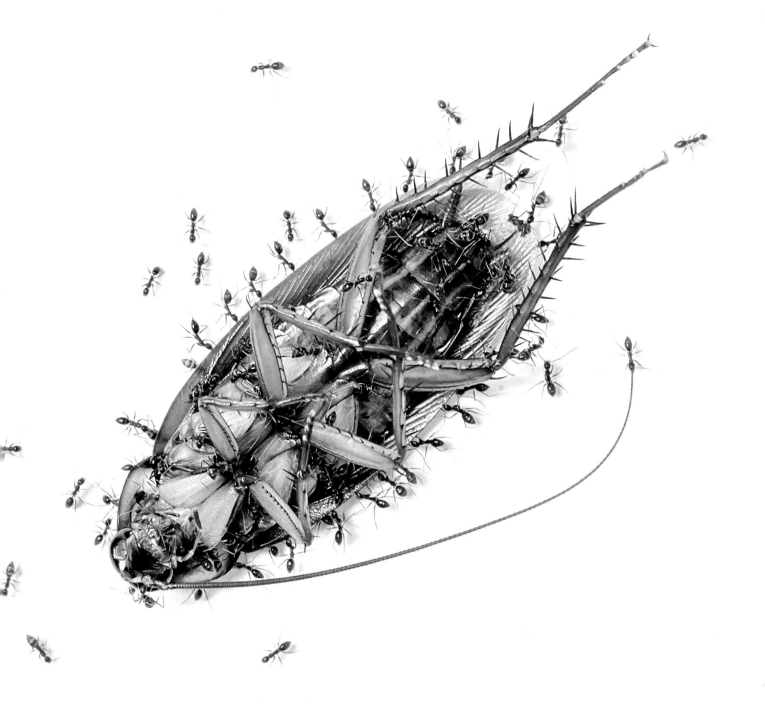

WHAT DO ANTS DO?

Black worker ants live for up to a year.

Worker ants spend their entire lives working. Their main job is to find food for the queen and her larvae.

A queen ant lives much longer than a worker ant. She can live for up to 28 years, but her whole life is spent laying eggs.

An army ant queen can lay up to four million eggs in a month!

HOW DO ANTS HELP?

These ants are tucking into a tasty apple that someone has thrown away.

Ants help to keep things clean! They help to get rid of rubbish by eating things we've thrown away.

Ants also help new plants to grow. Some plants make seeds that are covered in a tasty oil that **attracts** ants. Ants feed this oil to their larvae and then bury the rest of the seed. The seed then grows into a new plant.

AMAZING ANTS

Giant Amazonian Ant

The giant Amazonian ant is the largest ant in the world. It can grow up to four centimetres long!

Bulldog ants live in Australia. They have a powerful **venom** that they use to kill their **prey**. They also have a painful bite.

Bulldog Ant

There are over 12,000 different **species** of ant in the world.

FUN FACTS

There are about one million ants for every one human on planet Earth!

Bullet ants live in rainforests. They are called bullet ants because their sting feels like being shot with a gun.

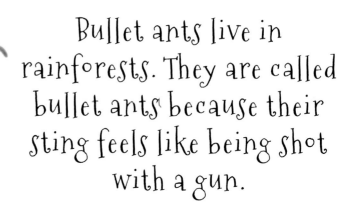

Ants are one of the strongest creatures in the world in relation to their size.

No ants here!

Ants can be found in every **continent** on the planet, except for Antarctica.

GLOSSARY

attracts	causes to come closer
chambers	large, underground spaces or caverns
cocoon	silky cases spun by larvae for protection
continent	a very large area of land that is made up of many countries, like Africa and Europe
fungus	a type of living thing that includes mushrooms and mould
larvae	young insects that must grow and change before they can reach their adult forms
mate	a member of the same species that an animal has young with
prey	animals that are hunted by other animals for food
species	a group of very similar animals or plants that are capable of producing young together
venom	a harmful substance that is injected through a bite or a sting

INDEX

24